TELEGRAPH

TELEGRAPH

KAYA OAKES

PAVEMENT SAW PRESS
OHIO

Editor & Layout: David Baratier
Associate Editor: Sean Karns
Cover Design: Lance King
Duck Logo: Joe Napora
Cover Art: Yoon Lee

The author would like to thank the following people: Andrew Demcak, Alex Green, Mark Cabasino, R. B., Brenda Hillman, Jeff Johnson, Jonathan Loucks, Ted, Sam Hurwitt, Betsy, Robert, Christine, Victoria and Lois Oakes, everyone from Kitchen Sink, my College Writing colleagues, and Sage Baggott.

PAVEMENT SAW PRESS
PO Box 6291
COLUMBUS OH 43206
http://pavementsaw.org

Full length books are available through the publisher or through:
SPD / 1341 Seventh St / Berkeley, CA 94710 / 800.869.7553
Literary journals and chapbooks are only available through the publisher

Winner of the 2005-2006 Transcontinental Poetry Award Editor's Choice for an outstanding first-book collection of poetry or prose. We read yearly from June 1st until August 15th. Send SASE for more information.

Pavement Saw Press is a not for profit organization, any donations are greatly appreciated and are considerered as charitable tax donations under section 501 (c) of the federal tax code.

Paper Trade: ISBN 978-1-886350-43-4

CONTENTS

ELEKTRA IN THE OFFICES

Barefoot and ripe with new embarrassment
Elektra walks up three floors, trying not to sweat

Constriction in her thighs, those red bands drawn tight
and everyone who waited without knowing her was blind
would receive her in a spotless blackness reserved
for those who have forgotten seeing means we learned to feel
in blindness, too.

You ought to have gone with her, years ago.
That was when it was easier to feel through things
by pulling those last strands of someone's hair

and wrapping up your fingers with them, like a tourniquet.
Elektra cuts her hair in bathrooms where her shape is strange
where the windows stay shut, even on the hottest nights
nail scissors in half-drunk bathrooms where she doesn't live.

While shots go off outside, the scissors scrape and pull.
She climbs the stairs climbed so many times before.
She has no one on her side,

she has handwriting and flowers gathered
in a backyard where her scalp burned pink
while the afternoons fed anorexic evenings
and the day's fluorescence never dimmed;

unsure, unripe, unready. Still the pounding rocks her steps
as innocents file past her. One hand, one knife,
one brother burning somewhere in the city,
The man is upstairs, working,
or failing at his work and practicing his oaths.
But nothing stops the inevitable click
of the door that yields to business.

7

ELEKTRA: A GIRL WHO LOVED THE COLOR RED

It seemed to bleed you, every night
those walks past the chapel, just so far apart
that we meant nothing. Your back
against mine told me nothing but the color gray—

and gripping that I wondered if it hurt
to turn toward another voice
another round of questioning.

As a girl, I loved my parents well enough
or at least they taught me tolerance.
But when they died, I loved them better;
so well that those tanks rolling into town

could never hurt me in the presence of my father's ash.
I would bend to stranger's shoes
and ask them if their laces meeting would bring back
that orb of suffocation, family.

Or better yet, bring back your sad and sightless eyes
so black I lost their center.

Elektra in New York

Natchios, the family name, does not so much fall off the tongue as skid across the teeth, an interruption in the scheme of things. Bullseye.

Yet you swung into nights girded with something beyond my capacity.

Sometimes, you were pacing neighborhoods where you had been a boy, a
	shortstop
blotting the diamond's symmetry.

I armed myself in red. The air between your misplaced kiss and the suction of the door opening; it took the wind right out of us.

Bullseye. Natchios was a target, nothing more, magnates in double-breasted coats, tyrants sketched on vases so old and fallible they remained locked up for generations.

I unlocked something, finding you, and guiding you in daylight when your worsted wools and fine-gauge cottons met between my thumbs. At your back, I knew how to push a moment so that it stretched, and tethered us, forever.

And when I died, it was maybe, what if, less than finite

And perhaps less than the things with which we filled ourselves.

FOREIGN CITY

I could have recalled cascades of hills, the swift breaking
of oaths made curbside while the work subsided indoors
or the way you crossed the park, head down, fists tight;
and maybe on the few best days, you walked shoeless,
a fool, making your way to churches where you gawked.

But fractures made in adolescence run so deep
that the image I had of you is irretrievable,
and you cannot wake and stride across those gaps
the ones made by the faultlines in this place we lived,
the one you didn't choose.

At best, when we crossed the bridge it was a passage to
a foreign city; cigarettes in the front seat I was not allowed
to smoke. Hoisted onto bars before I could really read
my sensibilities were innate, and dangerous as fiction
which was really all I understood, of this city and of you

But when you lost your sense of color and only managed
seeing blue and green, maybe I became your eyes, and am them still;
myopic, tipsy, skewed at best. At least still a stranger crossing the bridge
that enabled you to be a better person, free of us.

EVERYONE IS DUMB

From you, the rich and wide
expanse of earth, spread out across
the country's waist. Inside the belt
that holds you fast, things churn;
inheritances of dank
and worm-wrought floorboards, the dusty
windows of a house
shut for seasons, boarded
against the bitterness of breathing.

From you, debris of ages
chipped and gouged. Celluloid
plots, too nefarious and convoluted
to be re-told in some coherent form;
discussions of character, running through
evenings when we stayed tight inside,
things outside us turning purple, black.

There is something to be said for what
is handed down: the brains, the green
behind our lids, our clamped and clumsy
tongues. Language wandered down to me,
came from where you turned it off,
a spigot wrenched too tightly.

On the label of the Yukon Jack bottle, a man survives by drinking underneath an ice-encrusted tree. A dog curls by his side, also surviving. You loved ice, but I never understood it. Spoiled by California, I wondered what it felt like, and brought home thermoses full of snow and mispronounced the names of places constantly, while you corrected me. *Oo-Zoo-Mit-Tie. Because the people who came before us said so.*

But the time before we lived here is, at best, remote. I imagine where the offramp fell in the late eighties, your grandparents' house teetered on beams that would have rotted thirty times by now. And now their street wears shopping carts around its neck, wrapped there like the cheapest jewels. When they lived there it wore Model As and wondered if Satchel Paige would bring the world right down around them.

Your people were very small. They might have been that way because they felt the smaller that they were, the less they intruded on this new world that didn't need them. And yet they overtook it: felons, gamblers, wives,.wrong reasons in the wrong place, and nothing here reminds you of them; perhaps the cemetary where your spinster aunts lie waiting for their grooms.

And they had groomed you, only boy, to be the very husband. But you chose north and women forged in a different furnace: black hair, green eyes, their roots in middle states: their thicker, even tougher waists; their arms like long-boiled hams: dimpled, warped and tough.

My Parents, 1956

She would have worn the pinker dress,
its foam around her knees in dirty movie theaters.
A boy's jitters in spectacles, a treble clef
wound tight like midnight mass
while his father waited with a strap.

My father's ears were seashells
from a shore far too familiar to me now
to be anything but alien, or crammed with twitching
déjà vu. My mother's dress was made at home,
frill and flash, hook and eye, too modest in the telling.

Her balance gone, those skewed eyes
honed toward anything but what they wrought together—
nightly rage, recombination, agendas
buried under mattresses
their bodies nearly burst.

In 1956, things begin like this—
a church behind them, the flaccid surge
of the Pacific, pushing though their confrontations.
The spelling out of children's names;
what loss when all those letters blurred
into the shape of overwhelming marriage.

WIFE

Hypnosis of construction
lights. The bridge that would never
finish building itself, half-span
flung out into the water pounded down.
Cables crossing over her head. The trophy wife
in diaphanous and variegating shades of green.
Palms flexing against the girders. Half of her

committing suicide. Half is in the limousine,
old glass and those construction lights.

The span returns her to her source.
Beauty that fades. Money that is spent.
Beauty's cheapest, after all. It's character
that costs you.

The incandescent wife. The lucent wife, the wife who turned
the other way. All wives are one and pulsing

flapping flooding out of being.

Grandfather is very tall, and has been dead
almost a generation by the time I manage to be born. I am very tall as well, and
I become an awkward thing when I am around my smaller father.
Grandfather was swift, wielding his cufflinks and ancient, rusted handcuffs.
        A prisoner of wrists.

My father tells me I am above average in many ways, but my wrists will
never match me in this surge toward superiority. They will forever be
the most fragile thing about me, so very small that every watch I wear
must have new holes punched in it by the leather-goods repairman, so that
        bracelets rattle up
and down my arms each time I reach for something.

While I retreat into the room reserved for girls, my father shrinks until
I cannot remember what it was we saw in him. He lacked grace, which,
unfortunately, I do as well. He hurt himself, compacted while his belly
grew, so that those pale, delicate legs might have barely meant to hold him up.

This contrast between small and large; the strength we've lacked from
birth, brick walls of hips, the smoky, shimmering myopia of our not green,
not brown eyes? Since Grandfather, we have mostly been waiting to go
blind, or, like Grandfather and Daddy, to drink from and get bottled up in
amber.

When I was young, I found stones in which insects had been trapped. These
were lined up on the windowsill, along with dolls whose slender waists I'd
        snapped
in bouts of fury. Now I know those flies and spiders
                        were really Irish men.

VICTORIANS

Do you remember working. Well.
A morning wasn't, you didn't think;
you went out. And it was cold there, would
you say you hated it. Hated.
It used to freeze your eyes shut, tears.
We didn't know salt water. Got cut your blood
would freeze, your spit.

Your children. The morning was the worst.
Their arms were like that, repetition. What was left.
You call it working. But you weren't alone. No,
not alone. It isn't always there, when someone is.

Tell me about the city. There wasn't one.
No hills no windows. No glass. What
did you see through. You saw through yourself.
Fourteen of us lived, out of seventeen or eighteen.
The luxury in that was leaving.

And then you came to the city. Then I came.
And you were better there, that's not
a question, you already have the answer.
You can't ask what you already know.

Alright, there were frames, and windows.
Explanations for things. Labor.
I taught Latin. The work never changed.
It was us being changed by it. And then you went
to Greece. I hated the ships. When we got to the Acropolis,
I laid down on the steps.

Olympia

I lived in this city full of stupid objects
And glorified rounds of pass the police, cringing

Where everyone was short and wide and full of notions
Ready to begin their movements, brief as manifestos

In the bar, after the owner's heart attack, everything
We absorbed was put on credit cards for later

And the man then sleeping next to me had holes
In all his T-shirts he'd put there for ventilation

Every house had coffee cans filled up with sand
Upon their porches, behind each screen door

A band was playing "Hallelujah," without
Its drummer (there were only three in town

And they rotated between living rooms like specters
Of necessity); on the bus each morning I would sit

Next to a girl named Catherine, whose shoulder
Read "Daddy" in sparrow-blue swirls of irony

Banners like sailors from the past, she put on
Shows in her garage and people drove in from towns

With complicated names huffed up with consonants:
Puwallup, Tacoma, Bend. In a freeway-side bungalow

Someone spiked my drink and I woke up in someone's car
While my boyfriend was taking punches to the face

On bets, and we went home with pockets full of bills
No comprehension of denomination or what it might have meant

To allow ourselves some "spending money", as I pushed frozen peas
Against his face and made collect calls to Berkeley

Announcing that we'd birthed, at last, our own manifesto
Which, by the time I hung up, had vaporized just like a smudge.

LIVING ROOM

1.

Boats crush the ocean. In the meantime,
I burn out my funk with white noise
and the television. Later,

I turn the one-eyed car around. This is
a flat world. There is an end to it. You

are on the margin of it now, falling quick
past the horizon. I point away from you
propelled toward the solitudes of pure distraction.

2.

And loved you for a day or two,

bathwater going lukewarm out of
too hot. You played music in the living room. In
the water, my body played its own shrill trick;
trying hard to reach that blackness,

to see that line of demarcation, the one
that splits me. The ugly and the bad. The vulgar
and the Protozoic. Your back
was half hairy and half clean. Sometimes
you crushed me in your sleep.

ISLANDING

There are voices, voices...
              John Berryman

In particular his disdain for efficiency;
the putting away. He can't manage. Islands of him
have skirted the edge of her bed —

mess of him closing in nightly.
She wants to be in it, his isosceles triangle. Each
corner to own her, banging hard on the edge.

The shoreline, the shoreline. Oh go ahead sing it.
Fuck efficiently cropped hard hanging niceboys, you
were the jetty; you were the clothes pooling out

on the floor. One day's shirts and pants melding
into the next one. She catalogues these things,
ferreting, secreting. She catalogues him.

CONSTRICTIONS

Life in this time, you
walking, bound by fabric
leather, elastic

cuffs of your sweatpants and lines
of your bra, breasts that fall loose
when you bend to retrieve

books, dirty in stacks. Life
in constrictions, hairs
duty-bound to curling

ironed to flatness, nesting
in patches—angled with razors.
Underneath these, the head

does its thinking. You are
taut in your kind of
irreconcilable beauty. Those thoughts of

looseness. Not naked but
covered by things that aren't
tight. He lifts his weights in

the kitchen. Muscle.
You pour out of your body, loose
waves of skin.

After sleeping, the morning. Drinking
coffee, binding your thoughts up.
Such tightness of mind. Feathers on the end of

the arrow. Constructed
for flight. Maximum
distance. Let fly they

land, poking the target. And buzz with that
taut hum of puncture.

On your feet, after rising, you make
the same sound.

When you live obsessed with roads, the way in is always elusive. A troupe moves, circuitous, without destination. Motion key to place. The most frightening part of freeway travel is entering the stream of cars. The movement overwhelming, distance impossible to gauge. Kneeling in the rest stop, the map uncreased, unwieldy. Knowing that moments from now, the sluggish car will force its way back in between the faster vehicles and make its pace. And pace is gain, and earning.

Before he went out the door I remember not much. Just fuzz or static, something like the noise between stations, or Montana when we drove for days and found nothing on the radio, maybe the faint, impossible noise drifting up from Arizona. Diné, my mother said, tensed and ready. She kept Piki bread from Hopi ovens in the freezer, thinner than paper and explosive at the touch. The Navajo sent language up from reservations where we'd passed in flannel shirts. I saw a dead dog at the roadside, ignored by a cluster of Indian kids, flies and maggots in its eyes. Everyone in my family goes blind, eventually; grandparents filmy gaze on holidays, cataracts to counteract what they don't want to look back on. The Indian kids stared back.

I think we were marked by something greater than where we came from. Maybe it was farther back than my parents could remember. They unfolded things to show us where we'd traveled, the van a mosaic of places left behind—barreling, sometimes, but more often wrecked and smoking on a roadside where we'd hitch our way to strip-mall towns in semis, inevitably driven by a man who'd fondle sisters' knees.

We were always breaking down. The intersection ought to have been called a landing place, but was less than that—a marker somewhere in West Oakland where the Irish great-grandparents tangled up in what was then a ghetto and is now a ghetto, ghetto on ghetto, a marker somewhere in Whiskeytown where the Dutch great-grandfather thrust a shotgun in his mouth, the ranch now underwater, a marker in Aptos where the great-grandfather milked a cow and let it kick an eye out, never even ducked.

We had been tough, and cities made us not as tough, though the women in the album are as broad as redwoods and might have been able to wrestle down genetics had the need for five square meals daily not defeated them. Their arms round like histories. And we all had things to differentiate us; I never attempted to stop growing until I outstood my parents, even knotted up on father's lap in photos my legs outstretched the frame. We were wrecked and we were stopping, inappropriately; everything around us matched the wreckage in the engine. Only subtle markers showed us where we'd been.

BENIGN CONDESCENSION

The need to be realized in a cluster of opposites.
Conservative elements circled the room
in their brightness. I am repelled by fragmenting,
yet desire it so astutely, I might
cut off all my hair. You had this plan which involved

splitting the building, shaving it down until
its storied history had been compacted

back to ground level. We would retreat
to the basement. There, enacting scenes from King Lear

there is enough history for us to begin.

The need for abandonment before it's completed. Whose
world *is* this? Fingers bent backwards so far
it looks like they're breaking, but in the meantime everything
looks good from here; it's as if
we were roofing some six story building.

You will fall slowly, as if the impact
cost you everything, you will be falling
through that propane-scented air.

The body goes from 0 to 100 in an eyeblink.

As if those figures matter when you're writing the check.

The need for objects to have their insomnia.
The dresses stayed awake all night, seducing you
on their battered wire hangers.

In the morning nothing fits.
Cars have shrunk, workplaces expanded.

There used to be room. Things took over,
archipelagoes of abandonment. They have worn out
their welcome and are now wearing rejection.

It looks good on them, a shade of reddish brown.

The need for his benign condescension. He likes.
He dislikes.

The need to contradict everything every time. Arguing into
the voicebox, whose words go unanswered? Let's fight
about nothing, let's get our teeth in it.

Let's get busy. You know,
this moment materialized before I could get here, fake sweets
and Bob Dylan, so I'm last in this line. Climbing the streets
where the streets went on up, we get to the top of them
only through effort. The surprise of that, suddenly. The reward of that,

standing, twisting out from the cities. Those truths we left
unstated, your occlusion. Your novelty would have worn off
if it weren't for the purity of that, the earned eccentricities

worn like a black dress, like a ship's prow.

TRACTABLE

this trouble coursed its way through torsos,
lodged itself in upper arms. in tendons;
ears pitched for greeting and a song.

the singer raging "forget you";
for god's sake he deserves it.
this trouble locked in upper arms, in triceps
he pushed his way off of the bed.

light flare let's flee; *no water,*
only rock. speed through that desert flocked
with shell casings, with flowers, with cactus pears
whose syrup smears our chins

this shrine chipped out of sand

a swell unfolding, a courtly love takes time
before it dies. the quandary's in her way
of making friction when she snuffs that chill,
the singer stranded in his saying. When she pushes, it is total.

When he speaks, there is no knowing.

VOLATILE

Against the trompe l'oeil of restaurant walls
you make beauty out of skin and painted ivy,
fingers chording D, toes turned inward—
Buddy Holly in your bony gristle, symphonic
as the dispossessed, morning's waifs
who kiss you late, jaded as this cruel and boring city.

Girls heading home at dawn, thin skirts
against their thighs, icy scalps that shine
through center partings in their hair. Boots
on curbs, jackets left in stranger's cars—
yours and asking, slipping past those curtains
in the angling sun.

Before I turned pale as disappearance
you may have seen me smoking in your entryway,
scarring mirrors with mascara, getting closer
to the idea of marking.
Resting then against your mailbox, now in bed.
Glamour's traces run the hemlines of my dress,
the one that swept the story from your doorknob—
erasing fingerprints, but nearly always leaving scars.

Point Guard

Had you given the assignment, her voice might have not
have been at home for me, waiting. *Are you being like
a good girl?* We are bad Buddhists,
we crouch into unhappiness like the linkage between fencewires;

in this picture she was home and nowhere near
like a good girl; needless to say a girl...

but my tank top would have been firm
against my monkey-hanging collarbone. You would have been pointing
just past me, toward the dwarf maple which grows out across
O St., pointing with your bad _____, promiscuous
as a white boy. Girl? Girl? I have paired myself

off with her: not because she suits me, but because she don't.
She calls me again to ask me what I'm being. We're fourteen
and the world is twenty-seven, and you are playing basketball—

a bad hat in a field of barren heads.

had to force it, you had to take your turn. So I learned to play, in cheap and peeling sneakers made for blacktops, the dust around my brother rising as he knocked balls through neighbor's windows, my hand lost in a stained and sweaty mitt. When the panes cracked, the splintering glass would hover for a moment: fragments of the things we saw through, when we sat and watched.

The people on the block were old, except for us, the only children on that block of rot, the houses in ice cream pastels, the yards landscaped from sacks of Quickcrete. But our front lawn remained, defiant in its weedy splendor, and in the summers, like every other girl growing up broad and tall inside my family, I played baseball like a clumsy fool.

When we made the trip to Cooperstown, we drove. Two or maybe three weeks on the road, going the long way, up through Canada to break out of the unforgiving landscapes of my Mother's youth. My father hated the Midwest like he hated Fernando Valenzuela, the Dodgers' fat and wheezy pitcher. I'd been stretched out in the back since Oregon, puking road-sick into paper bags.

In thick eyeglasses and shiny shorts, my sisters squinting through lank lengths of hair, we played against the Mexicans from down the street, their advantage handsome sons, their disadvantage being even thicker than we were. When I was at the plate, I couldn't see the outfield; mole-blind from reading my way through summer evenings, wondering if I could bunt it toward their rotund mother, who dropped everything that came her way.

It was better in the stands, at minor league games, where the drink choices were Bud or Chablis with a hard c-h, and the afternoons laid down and stretched out like the feral cats who wandered through the outfield stands; those hunters, alert to everything that spun toward them. We dozed into our sunburns and dreamt of the off-season, when we'd move indoors to hockey rinks, or wander through the blasts of wind at Candlestick Park, where we always lost the van among the Civics. Willie Mays had just retired; McCovey's hooded gaze would coat the outfield in a base hit. The stands would thin, and we would thin with them, cluster of puffy jackets, discounted blue jeans, the happiness it gave my father, like nothing else, when we rode home like victors, our contribution little more than awe.

1988

Antagonist, didn't we
always neglect one another so beautifully
that strangers tripped on their curbs just
to gawk? I love you antagonist, not the one, blot.
Shifts go on around us, the room swallows light,
solidifies, creeps back to a still.
Lady leans onto a table she knows is smeary.
Lady smokes. Lady wants so bad to be known
as insouciant. I love you stain, creep,
indignancy. Runaways bend to sidewalks
they know are sooty. Runaways smoke.
Runaways want so bad to be known
as splinters gone free of the relevant life.
Lady will affect a bourbon and soda.
Lady leaves rooms with a smirk. Runaways
greet her, out on the tiles, on the strip
between splinters and lightning, between shatter
and desperate kiss under desks.
I love you, antagonist, so wrong
for the system. Lady plays 1988 loud on the stereo,
splinters her hands with guitars. Runaways ply the sidewalk with
power chords, work the angles, feel lonely in cities,
creep back into towns.

Antagonist, isn't it all about waiting?
Between years, we got prettier, easy
to taste, smoother with continents buzzing our skin.
Between years we learned the lesson of begging,
chipped our front teeth on doorknobs,
rubbed hard on each other, the table, the ground.

SANTA PRUDENCIA

In a bikini on the bed the body heaved and then let go—
truths come one by one, punctual as weakened batteries.

It's not going to be enough, this siesta. There is an absence
in the present tense. An active missing

that runs constantly throughout the actions
we don't do.

Going out to see how the sky
would lean into me, after I had

forced such forgetting of it, painting it
in diagrams. Here. A water-colored soul.

The money that you carry could never make you
what you are. The absences that I paint out

in purple washes are just me becoming.
Without a face sometimes I think you forced the sky.

Our lives, our matching body temperatures, are absolute in flickering.
Our lives briefer than prayer candles, seven-day flames.

Saint Augustine

Before me, my sisters moved like minor goddesses: full hipped and garbed in Catholic skirts, plaid and pleats receiving messages from deities we understood to be benign, but who inevitably failed us. I'd remind myself that to believe in Him meant believing in salvation, but salvation meant you fell down like a fool at recess, that you fell and bled because He said so. Like innocents we stuck our tongues out daily.

Being a sister meant being a part of repetition. As in *we've seen your kind before. Your kind* meant that weird mix; the one that never adhered to the test strip, like the blur of base and acid, pink on yellow, meeting somewhere in between. The one before me, seven years older, wore stockings underneath her skirt and suffered runs in them; before that, another burned the halls, some combination of beauty and genius that faded everything around her back to grey. How much in the seventies was grey.

Outside those classrooms, parents' friends went headfirst into rice paddies. We were bewildered by this Christ, this spook who walked beside us in our communal gowns; eleven virgin brides and fourteen virgin grooms in ties so tight they fainted at the afternoon procession. In front of the Virgin's statue on the playground, I vomited my breakfast watermelon, imagined those black seeds I'd swallowed against mom's wishes were the beginnings of vines; vines that might have grown through asphalt and managed to bear fruit: however meek, however wanting.

MULE

I am becoming you; inhabitable lorry
On shuddering wheels. I pull you through
Rajasthan, pull you through Dar Es Salaam.

You feed me
from your hand; raw grains, coagulated honey.

And say you love this. Your big body
in the carriage, my form bent

and pulling. And you say one day
not so far off, when I have weakened
you will pull me.

We will arrive. We will arrive in places that are
inhospitable. We will descend. We will
be beggars without bowls for alms, without
waxed·takeout cups.

We will be jaded by then.
We will be the same sad flesh.

Logical Fallacy

Childhood songs about baby bumblebees, drowning girls, golden warriors and loss of limbs. The grimacing of faces when the teacher turns the page. Across the room from her, I sat in a corner, punished for neglecting to wear panties on the first day of school.

The songs of childhood are not grim, but filled with minor fourths and keyed so they stay in your ear; a little wanting noise to wake the sleepers, late at night, a threnody like that first awareness of the impermanence of things. In our backyard, our patch of concrete surrounded by a scrubby hedge, I found a salamander, calcified with weeks or maybe months of sunshine on its slithery form. I found my father crying when I brought things up; his lack of siblings, his dead parents, the absence in his family of cousins, uncles, aunts.

The one about the ladybug. She'll fly away home, and find her children gone.

Reservoir

We hit this shoreline in darkness. To begin.
This is a half-reported note from land. No one
here remembers their home country. My partner
is a half-mute stranger with brambles
in his hair. Our assignations taking place behind
rotating backs of blank-eyed enemies.

I cabled mother from the shelter. *Could you
come retrieve me?* But I have no father; no mother
then, no country. A stalking sound I make sometimes
in morning hours, pacing through these ghettoes.

Some decades back an infant crawled from its
infirmary. They blew
her fingers off and left her there to paint their buildings.
Holding the roller in her shaky baby teeth, she became me.
Now blind in starless, non-electric night,
remembering the vomitoriums
and Peugeots of the hotwired ruling class.

The whining, ending lives. The world a spherical mess;
our cleaning led to barrenness.

PORTRAIT OF THE PARTY AS A GIRL

First we took the leader
palpated him and sometimes turned him over;
the lawlessness, the new decrees
by us, for us, or something like that. Maybe

he shrank and maybe he grew, but aware
that things had changed, we were
lost as to what to do with him.

So we took the capital, the trains,
freeways underneath us spitting dust

so we took the air and pieces from the sky,
water all around us, the leader
mute upon our backs.

And we grew convex with our possessions,
things denied us for so long we felt our sense
of ownership cascading. At night, one of us sometimes

feeds, has conversations with him.
These days he is as soft as breath, white-chested
and full of tepid stories. When we stop, we lay
him down between us. Now
that we are with him always, we
no longer think of rest.

Seven Brides

We lived inside a stinking tint, halfway between black and brown
and nothing left. Shelter was the foolish hint of windows open,
facing east. Each morning, we were blind to one another.

We ate like it was madness, never enough. A root
would rise up from our throats and fork in our clogged mouths.
Speech was permissible, as long
as understanding never clouded it.

Rhythms played in school were false. But she
commands them as we're taking turns
compressing in her wedding gown. Size five;
almost tight enough to make you dizzy.

I'm going to put it on tonight, drive
my broken car against the hills. You ought
to see the way it looks on us, various pasts
enmeshed across the ugly scale of satin,
our eyes a cloud of hungry bees, humming just beneath the veil.

The Renaissance

A time when everything we said required context
and our neighborhoods were filled with a silence that was absolute.

I heard you waking hours after I had left the house,
heard movement in the rooms I'd abandoned in favor of
compassion fatigue, serving out the needs of others
wherein I grew as green as trees peeled free of layers of disease.

An epoch of encircling moons that stratified us
even as we worked to name them. The season was a summer,
failing still to quit, even after it had worn on us, bleached us
until we faded into shadows baked on sidewalks, those heel prints
of the passengers who moved through this, our time

meeting and creating divots in the narrow confines of our necks.

Behind the school there lay another school, and in that school a series of smaller schools, like the Russian dolls that he brought back from Alaska, their husks peeled off to reveal their smallest daughters, snuck inside.

In every classroom there were occasions to dress up, a kind of finery I could not have imagined when I saw it imitated on the block at Halloween; the teachers braceleted up to their elbows, the veiny rocks the most valuable, the boys fringed and the smallest girls with their hair twisted up like butterflies. The purple velvet shirts, their bishop sleeves miraculously free of dirt; the prairie skirts in layers like confections. The dancing moved so slowly it was as if nothing was going to make it speed up, ever, and all around the dancing, the singing pitched in waves.

In California he was driving miles and miles, returning to her, while she integrated her way into cultures that were as distant from her childhood as the languages of playgrounds were distant from my studied, cultured tongue. And at the school, my mother teaching urbans, as they were called, my sister and I played at tribes, the game of first day ice-breaking. Those names. Paiute. Chippewah. Coeur D'Alene. I could not speak it forcefully. *My tribe is Irish.* Only my mother and I blushed to red.

Fucked in Four Parts

Dhukka

We are getting at the root; this time,
among clawhammers, acoustic punk--

dusty shrines to mark the corners.
The birth, just unexpected. Rush-hour
McDonald's. A tray
of french fries and her water breaking.

Cheeseburgers bursting tissue on the slick floor.

Recollection of a virtue. Life went.

Wednesday at 12:15 the aneurysm.
Body cremated, according to a mumbled two-part list.

"Burn me. Burn me and forget it."

Wish List

Brink of remembering. It envelopes
and then surrenders. Regrette-rien! And then the toll plaza,
forked lanes and different music
to resound from every booth. The bald man
takes a dollar with a snap. Turning
the radio, her collar is the shape of pyramids;
money at your neck. The eyeless triangle conveyed.

Oh San Francisco. Riot of mariachis
in bellbottoms, tofu
burritos and tequila sunrise, ribboning across the bar.
We danced a little; a rhythmic
foothold in the dank oasis.

If I could have one thing, baby, it might not be this.

Tequila Sunrise

Ribboning the water; was that blood?
I laugh a little bit too hard, she anticipates
a recollection. Things will

come back to her. As in
rotundas, the curvature of roofs mimicking our skulls.

Dia de los muertas and the platform boots
that made her too tall to match her new I.D.

You cannot come in and have a drink here,
but you can linger at the door, your
lush petalling a little bit obscene.

Santeria

The rest went off. Tirades, after six drinks,
won't last long, will become contrivances.

And every time the phone goes off at three,
I picture him, dog-eyed among his fingered pages.
Her, laughing, earrings swaying near the chin.

What distance I had forced and keep on forcing.
Recalling conversations that spun out
like ordinary wind; the fancy backyard where I smoked

and let him into it. My life. That gross serenity
I did not earn.

Always Coming Second

A body I didn't ask for
and everything that kept me up at night, the lines
across the morning faces that meant what sunlight leant them;
after the cases had been packed
and the talking put away for later.

The first played on the beak of a boat:
Alaska, the Bering Strait. In an over-hot jacket
the water went under me, steel and new-banked snow
severed by fins.

Seven years old in some sister's coat
the best I could do was to hold out
a fistful of candy, toward that
soggy brown hair and guitar.

The second wrote on his jacket with markers
tracings of pot smoke and dullness in classrooms,
rumors of red hair, strung over his shoulders,
a rope I clung to like it could pull me back.

Fourteen in plaid skirt and bad skin in the back
of the school vans that ferried us, over winding hills
a wavering coming up from his throat
something like Led Zeppelin or Megadeth
under my fingers.

The third carried an amplifier up my narrow stairs,
and I played the bass through it along with Who albums
lost in the hallways of upstairs
and he ran off with a freshman girl so tiny

the top of her hair aligned flush with his nipples.
He wasn't the brightest thing, lost in classes
where polysyllabics flitted around
but after I read him *Kubla Khan* one night
he made a song that kept me awake until college.

The fourth was homeless, wore remorse
like a chain. Girls from school
would cruise him, conscious their knees
looked bigger the shorter they wore their skirts

I laid with him on the lawn of the empty
Greek Theater, ionics and dorics, twilight
on his cheeks, and later
he chased me through seven train cars while I panicked
and spun through explanations I never ended up giving.

The fifth ascended beyond tiny stages, beyond reputation.
You can find him in stucco and wristbands,

track marks and tattoos in an alternating
range, ex-wives and alimony bleeding his royalties
some afternoon's stink wafting up from his strings.

The sixth pulled and put me into my place
which, as it turned out, was rain-drenched, walking down
country side roads at 3am, toward a golden house with a cage
of lovebirds in the window, a history smearing in notebooks
under my arm. Out of all of them, he played guitar the worst:

tasted so bitter, hurt himself like it didn't matter.
Ten years later, a fifty-dollar phone call revealed
his parents were still asking what had happened to
that girl with the black hair who spread Crisco
on toast at the table and fell out of the picture like the gloss
on a mirror.

In California, the seventh decided to switch to the drums.
It was like forgetting the reason for melody, the reason for rooftops
where he'd hauled up couches and bong hits left me reeling.
Each morning, I'd wake in my dress between him

and his aunt. Thrum and thrum. Skins and sticks. In an alley
I kissed him in front of his girlfriend, then bent at the waist
and let loose the red wine that was boiling up my throat
to meet his salty, lost tongue.

Eight repaired Volkswagens, black moons
under his nails; blue grease on the counters when he'd
make a meal. Khaki overalls stained brown at the cuffs.
Like a lightswitch, a Russian crept into his bed
and awoke nine months later, mother and wife.

Nine and I burned down a thousand towns
between San Francisco and Tijuana,
with a Super 8 camera pressed to his thigh.
Driving was like revolving through doors opened years ago
only to find they had never stopped spinning.
Awake in the back of a truck with a mouth full
of moss, the morning really an afternoon lost
a case of fireworks under the seat
Negra Modelo on the beach, bursting siphons of clams;
detritus of starfish, littered over blue sand
and then New Mexico, Arizona, Colorado, Idaho—
a motel or a valley
feet frozen to the brakes;
a ticket handed down by a mystical trooper
in between orange meals and minutes of sleep.

Ten broke windows and slaughtered lambs
in his spare time. In between, his body laid out on the sofa
while gangster films rewound themselves on the VCR
then played again. And again, girls left messages
on our machine, and I went to work, where boxes piled up
and I moved them from one shelf to another
from one room to another, anticipating
Scarface berating Michelle Pfeiffer when I got home,
but then he'd sit at the piano and shatter everything.

Rapture convenes and dismisses us when in its midst
and then he went and broke my face
and it was over.

That unasked for body went and changed
wore a belly, learned to sag
and slept enough, then trouble faded
and semblances of what we made of one another
were painted on the walls, in that apartment
over a gas station at the intersection of the 24
and 80. And then he started crying every night
and the crying spread.

Windows open in the springtime let out weeping
until the diesel smell no longer stung
and I was carrying things out to the car before the sun came up,
like normal.

You asked me what I made of this,
charting patterns, making maps.
across them, all those hands played me between
choruses ground out like discarded wrappers, things
of beauty that were not recorded and thus became
the fleet, lost instinct of a momentary girl
who might have passed through music as if it were
her native domain. And you were strong enough
to lift me, and to lay me down, but what you wrote
never paused to second guess, so it was all rave and joy,
and never felt the boundaries of names:
All the songs you played were covers.

Huddled in phone booths
under overpasses intersecting, Xing out
the moon, the bass and I were last. He reminded me of suburbs:
The latency of streets that meet, yet never cross,

boys in uniforms parading home from baseball,
Girls who suck a dick at twelve and call it innocence.

But I made it mean too much, that undercurrent
essence of the things that move us, which we
forget in favor of the flash and flight
of frontmen. And when it meant too much, it meant
we were ruined in the front seat of
a station wagon, embedding one another's names
on one another's necks
And seven years have passed since then. I swear
I'd press against that sound again
even if it ruined me.

Always coming second;
crouched among cables and amps,
riding in a backseat next to puking girls who'd later
try to fit the dents I'd left, walking through
some greasy alley in a smoker's clothes
with black, or red, or silver hair—
Hadn't I put them second too? The ones who knew me well enough
to guess that I'd be waiting when the car pulled up
and took me with them, without thinking, without speech.

Or else I learned to smother words
so well that minor guesses might have found me just as dumb
as every other one who made a song compose itself
and felt that it meant something more
than the rapture of the backstage kiss, the stage-bound nod
or the dirty shirt worn into bed for months
like it was something better than we could ever be.

Seedtime

Each story is the indisposed
young body, which is going sick.
Within the sound a discourse and a getting back.

Each leaflet is a matter of that body's
tremulous health. You and I have hidden in the parapets

above the landmines, and below the helicopters.
You and I have willed our conversations

picking out these ecstasies, pointing toward
ourselves. Along the way the getting back—

handfuls of hair, a finger gesturing
blindly without means to beckon;

our childhood homes, our teenaged wallets.
The estrangement of your handwriting;
a coloring, a scrap. Beneath us

people eat hand grenades and powder
their last meals with creosote.

Above us, pilots get lost and find themselves
forever in air above the last edge
of the Atlantic.

We are alone, my love. Except for this
endless suspension between dirt and danger
and cutting blades in complex air, there is no life for us.

Only the severed clips of sound some through the windows

which we leave half open, revolutionaries
stranded in the stasis of our cowardice.

Telegraph Rep

Waiting, before being, you were waiting for me
before I came into a world, wrecked and wise.
On buttresses over Copenhagen we learned to smoke
and witnessed massacres of those we loved

while age took and throttled what we'd known of them
and one perfect tear would fall down your face.
You told me *age is meaningless*
and you were right about everything but that.

Little genius, Laurence Olivier may have brought out your sad side
or perhaps it was only the fact that the night
here doesn't begin, but fades out of the afternoon
as if it were Hamlet himself. Indecisiveness
may be something that runs in this family, witness
thirty-odd years spent roiled in confusion
and then maybe a premature death;
or even better, a long, drawn-out illness
that teaches us to look back through the rheum
and see only the trailers of movies, unrolling
A fracture of plot—

profile of a man caught between moments
when the course of his life had more than a meaning
and less than this series of consequences.

BLACKOUT SERIES

1

We made a sound like kicking
up through thickness that might have been water;
and after getting loose, you let me sleep.

2

Naïveté of being young:
I used to label it as something
to be grown out of, a little piece
of today's misery to irrigate tomorrow.

Another expectation, grandiose,
we were trained from birth to feel; that a little bit
of everything we made would carry over, because
we had a name for it.

3

But the nameless losses gathered up.
You could wear them like you wear
your bracelets into bed —
so cold your cuffs left imprints
on my waist, our breath
sketching illustrations between us when we woke.

4

There was nothing like excitement left.
Just dust and atoms, dust and dust.

LOVERS

One's own face begets another.

Wrong, I think, to be aroused by the crinkle-eyed visage
of my neighbor; the one who smokes behind the cypress tree,
counts off his little daughters, and goes inside.

Also the possibility that sex is loveless. Drunk,
he likes to think. Otherwise, he hates it;
the images inside his head like irritating, wingless bugs.

Late night, I rule the front yard with my cigarette.
His noticing. That comet rides the nightsky,
20th century bookend. *It rhymes with vomit,* I tell him, ridiculous.

So this must be apocalyptic lust. Approved by omens. Beginning
ending in freak circumstances.

Black coffee on the porch at two. Then children
are let into their houses. Caretakers
line this street, and every other morning gardeners
come out with gas-powered blowers

to clean it up. I manage celibacy
from time to time. Unthreatened by fidelity.

The hard part, though, is picturing
lovemaking when it snows outside. This seaside
basin with its ugly air will not allow it. Once,
I drove with boyfriend #6 to Arizona in December

made love in the front seat of a truck, no heater.
But here in California spring, there is no way
to hang that image up; cold steering wheel against the ass,
cold fights across the desert into Colorado.

Between two sides the street breaks up my vision.
There is a narrow place where I watch him at night,
receding back into his parenthood as if he were

a motel clerk. And me, long distance
truck driver, left thigh *that* hard from shifting.

THE UNIVERSE

Work was a room with just one window,
and every few years, the window moved, so that the view
while still the same, was slightly altered

only enough to fool you when you were obtuse.
Work was a room and there you lived, a pussycat, a grin
a thing that leveraged compromise and weakened alliances
for you were as sure and real as charm.

But the little movements are like spies
and go unremarked upon, and, perhaps, ignored.
and the papers that shift just enough for a promise
shift back when you turn to them. This might be your notice.

When you worked you learned that everything is compromise
that "want" and "need" are interchangeable as thieves
and what's gone might have been called desire
but is better labeled as unclean ambition

because the window moved enough
to promise it would always move.

BRINK

First persimmons, the angularity
of fruit displays incongruous against the teeth of tractors
that line every block. So you swear;

stars at six are just things up there to be counted —
rain for an hour, then brackish gutters and the sky.
Squat fruit; ugly, truncated stems.

It's nearly tasteless in the kitchen. There isn't time
to eat before the oracles
will contradict themselves. Orion dangling

above the library. Ugly shoulders, heavy legs.
Water shocks us with its will and sends us in.
You steady me. The mealy fruit is evening crashing.

My house's angles. Come through
the paradox of hot November, come fetch me
from the corners where I wait.

GUITARS

fat paragraphs and irreverent clouds with
the sun behind them

rods of light going from
behind to dirt

always jagged guitars amplified
through second-hand speakers.
I think about

the sound more often than I think
about the rhythm.

Migrated toward his hands.
Twelve-string ready for
the soft set. Purple pick in hand, the stage
just tilted enough...

If you sit still I'll get that
splinter out

and then we'll do it
again from the top. Go.

The boys were 16,16,15,16.
From the suburban gulag. Playing
for six months, worshipped
in Australia

she and I debated at the bar. Thinking
Neil Young and his descendants.
My bass and her astigmatism

"in a world without
guitars" she asserted. Then standing,
tuning hers to play
a song. *Cowgirl in the Sand.*

POINTILLISM

Each meager measure of time cuts across us. Slashing
our bodies up into sections which will not
be joined in this present discourse on eternity.

As much as I'd like it, it'll never mend up. Chunks
going off in that flagrantly sweet fashion. Nobody
completes us. We eat what we can in the meantime;

make our bodies up out of nothing, pretending
the methodology reaps what it lays down. In pajamas,
you wander the hallways inefficiently.

I lean on the bedposts, progressing in measures.
The pictures, when developed, all came back with smears.

TROUBLE WEATHER

When everything was wet, entire counties
slid into the ocean; speculation
about the state of hills was rife and loaded
with the tremors we'd been cursed and dampened with since birth.

But I loved the shaky state my mother
had forced me out into so long ago my skin was superannuated;
pocked and lined and folded like a map of destinations
shoved into a glovebox years ago.

And strangers sent me notes across the internet, fireflies
of speculation querying as to where my gifts had gone
notes that didn't warrant a reply, the ones
about the shame of lost potentials and the rages
snuffed out, one by one, the wet encroaching uselessness of art
gone sour, of words cranked out for purposes unknown.

Because, like the ground beneath me, I had had promise
and I had gnawed my nails to stumps
in spasms of the in-between; when nights closed over town
I fought them back by writing, and I fought hard enough,
sometimes, to vaporize the notion that the fight is cursed.

HUMILIATION BY DEGREES

Suddenly I was humbled by my bounty, unfamiliar
in the country; as if the lights on me had peeled,
jerked back, and set me forth.
Between infamy and discrepancy, the footpath marked
with steps I'd yet to take.

Abruptly I was standing with my arms full,
embracing objects as they were thrust upon me—
addled, lost, and yet as close to safety as I would ever come.

And something started happening

Between what passed for smarts but bound itself in worry;
between the shifting lights on the wall cast forth
by neighboring apartments;
between us in the rigors of householding;
between responsibility and action, in the midst of
frigidity and scathing heat

I was discovered, face up,
stomach toward heaven, my back bound to floors
that we steadfastly tried, and failed, to shine.

Fuel Cell

Habit of always descending into it. As if
recognition were possible solely beneath things.
You were a shade, patch stuck there on the sidewalk.
Your stigmata would open and close on your hands;

tiny mouths which were spitting out blood,
then holding it in. Spitting and holding—

My mouth on my wrist digging into it lightly.
That didn't work but biting down felt alright.
We were twin blight: never that hungry,
couldn't drink deeply enough.

Skunk brother, sun spot, memoir in the vacuum.
You are a problem I will never resolve;

you are ache and you are that royal insomnia.
And you make me strong. You make me so strong.

THRENOS

Another eye will have caught mine by the time
this ash has settled. Still in the evening,
your songs filter these dust-smitten hills—
raw land's perplexed lamentation as it shoulders our bodies,
afternoon's halftones
fading out to atonal. Under your breathing galaxies

have been known to do their thing
while you sing turbulent themes
into my neck's thick threads. Did it go inward;

that sparse recollection, saddest sliding lip, treble
barely moving those fine hairs against your ear. It may have
gone outward, bass in your throat, bass

casting its back note, hooking
my ankles to the floor; fires consuming
half of our city while we kiss through
bridges of unsteady song

oblivious to the universes
steadily being burned and born.

THE BIRDHOUSE

Just like that, and she would bend
and seed the travelers, then they would group
to move skyward against the sap of thought.

Everything was purple: the bank of aspens
rocking in winter afternoon, the husband's nose
interrupting the hallway to the kitchen; a loamy trail

back into those Berber rugs that tore my feet
each morning when the house awoke me:
the travelers bludgeoning themselves, one by one

against the ranch-house windows. This was the country,
more or less: absence of sidewalks, absence
of people who might have made the sloping steady;

objects arranged on everything: Chinese dolls, miniature
wooden horses with their wooden manes, a hundred children
ranged in pigtails, mouths clamped in anemic smiles

ornateness of the golden filigree spun
around the television, and at seven every night,
Jeopardy and a dull confusion

mistaken for sleepiness: just pills and age.
In haze, and black outside, a neighbor's
deranged rooster set it off at 9pm, exactly

and she would lead me into bed, the room
all white and frilled, the wedding cake
I would refuse to bite until I really wanted it.

Sleep Talk Believe

Rest of the alphabet, letters
we live through are vowels but
songs go in this manner:

x   y   z

Half step of a left hand and
bass end of the melody, ascends
c, c sharp, c, c sharp (and his fingers
play scales when he
isn't speaking): who you are and
how you say it

News delivered on
cassette, padded with
transparent bubbles.
The brutal end of the alphabet
serves.for this moment, the bitter
consonants spat out in a
half rain of unsaid

I am twisting in
this dance like a monument

Third thud of each eyes' gaze falling
separately onto the object. Albums dusty,
gnarled in their sleeves. Stellar
regions. Hora decubitus. Stella
by starlight. Bitches brew. Impressions

collected, an astral map.
Bent sideways, this head's origin—
Easter Island or Sacramento. No difference.

Worn down into sleep, cradled by
reeds and padded with trumpets, dreams
pull me through the cavity of the nighttime—

They make a place for the infant
before it arrives

and paint the room blue, trusting
in calm, faith in her belly

and I am the child, head back, hair
grazing bare shoulders, trusting
my father turning

the dial of the portable radio

He tells me Japanese see
that bright band in the sky and call it
the river of heaven.

╲ome worms turned in the wood.
A humming, followed by sweat.

Rain, we theorized as children
was either god's piss or
his tears. Now when
it falls from the night to
the night it is sweat:
alkaline, salt.

One dream fed into
the next one. The wood
rotted, the house veered left.
1/2 of an insect lay crushed in the pages.
Opened them and found its body
like a crab's back.

Tension between raindrops—oracular space.
The place where
voices move—antelopes.
Like worms turning in mulch, we
sleep, the moisture
sinking into our cheeks, our glands.

BOREAL

Passivity as a virtue among noise;
wanting to know someone and their
resistance; a tangled automation.

A shutter is a finger is a limb, frozen.

Shining in matte surroundings.
In the magazine, she photographs her lover:
the first date. Then two
weeks later. Now he leans into it:
hammered greys and faded blonde.

I was, I was, I did. The boys
poured fat into their coffee, thin streaks
of lipids, the butter of the photograph.
When I was the lens they did not know.

The image came back flat and limitless.

Stir two and keep your fingers crossed.
A pall to make your syrup sweeter, the sketch that lingered
on your tongue. All this sinking fruit
will not make up for how we lost it, biting through
the skin to wreck our frail teeth on the pit.

It chafed our taste like velvet; that was skin.
Eyes gone aubergine, your face trainwrecking, barely a fade.
I could have receded; the halfway screen,
the door that never asked. And asking why

how fooling is, the play of gaining information. A middle name?
A pleurisy, an Uzi spray of what-you-mean. This is left for weeks sometimes,
ooze of newer creases, bowl of over-ripenings.

The foolish thing. As easy now as splitting teeth,
as splitting velvet, and you have no mores. There are no bones
inside you, now you're waxing famous;

a name drops all it has in letters, a story read
but moral credence never learned. The palsy comes
with recompense; what we skip away from,
what we're scraping toward. I pull an eyelash free
and paste it to your mirror. This bracket for suggestion is
a tiny cuff you'll never see.

TRAJECTORY

I was born to consider the dazzling
array of stresses each morning
regurgitated from a dream, the clash and push in afternoons
as I watch teenagers' eyelids twitch. I have worn
them out again. They are full of metaphor.

I was born to reconsider ways of getting lost.
While my colleagues learned to work
because of work, and not because of meaning
I dug up the meaning from the work, revealing
ways of getting lost
and ways of being found again.

Responsibility slashed my birthing cord
and bound it up again before it could fully heal.
Because I was good at thinking, my rewards
were just like this: each morning's
rush to consciousness, a swift fist
to the chest that starts the thinking going,
and in the afternoon the fist is loosened
to be replaced by nods.

Repetition's middle name just might be valor
or perhaps she wears a shield and calls it willingness
to change. Whichever way you dress her,
she still goes out at night, coward in blue shoes,
the pitch of everything you said twisting around her like a skirt

and she will move despite stupidity, towards you
like a bandit through with thievery.

Memory stains us; when I wake at night
I walk the house, shoeless and dispapearing—
and when I lie back down again, it's as if
waking meant more to me than the possibility of sleep

because you wore me down past sleep, past waking.

EFFLORESCENCE

It was always a matter of patience between us;
brute rearrangement
of petals, tight flower
hibernating in the chest like a bridegroom.

Our worth discovered in pauses—
arrangement of distances, both finite and plain.
Between longing and motion the affable line.

We swear to each other it's private trouble.
It's internal pressure, not artifice, and not gloss.
We filter our half-smiles when we face one another.

Behind porch screens we are standing at odds.

You reveal what you can't know as you hang up the phone.
I sleep in surrender, all my cautioning gone. Glass breaks
underneath us while we turn to the side,
profiles at the ready, summer's breath at our backs.

That distance.
Hierarchy between speech
and what goes unspoken. That is where we rest,
where we argue and eat.
Where we concentrate, where we practice this love.

PERCIPIENCE

Postcards from the island of remorse,
slippery reminder that there is
a kind of self-love that grinds with us to forever.

Hands folded, as if in prayer; the pendant
that greened his neck. "Call a priest" —
instead she gleans him,

his dying in the city with its hotly coiling streets.
Once lost there they drank vodka over
Casio keyboards. Beyond suffering.

The singer's gardenia wilting in the bathroom
while the women piss. How peculiar, how new —
in spite of life, we live it.

———————————

But peonies. They unfurl, and every boy
who slept there would later call it
ripe. The flowers were one less a meal,

one more a mark to point the bedside table, low.
When he knew the ceiling sloped. He forgot
and then it leveled.

I am gauging this, I read the postmarks
as they come. Phoning after dark, when
you knew me least but wholly, your voice calls

"this one, this one."

———————————

Read & read & read.
Your fucked head resists this change.
It's not enough to push things in, hoping
they'll stand a chance, and stay.

Shove delight into the frame,

one storage box locked up
and swollen with this noise.
A drunk man's sweeter breath
will ventilate this aisle. How many words
fall out this way. When he finishes
the book, someone will have to come collect

and twist the remnants.

Poor

Typically, terror and boredom.
The arc of seasons as we fillet our way through
"the prosperous years." Pacing the confines, a radiance
engulfs us, but it isn't a particularly
beneficent one; it shakes the jism out of you,
it makes you wonder how it all got started—

I promise you
a bandit's kiss, I reach up from the makeshift shade
our promiscuity has left behind.

Your teeth are mailrooms where the clerks
will fall asleep while standing, your tongue
a ludicrous, enthralling bind.
A part of everything in me is precious
when I placate humming ghosts,
and close my svelte black wallet.

A part of you corkscrewing now
across the room's broad silence,
as if the stubborn gyrations of this world
were just a flicker in your vast eyesight.

When we can't prosper, well, we matter somewhat.
We might diminish. We might
get left behind.

Phenomenology

Listen, friend: our columns, labeled
perchance and *perhaps*, leave no room
for *definite*. Between the swellings
I wanted (you'll forgive me)
foetal exclusivity, research time
for my private rottings. A dying friend announced
"I'm dying", and we went to hell. Not such
a bad place, but the galleys of her memoirs
were waylaid by the succubi.

Empathy goes with the orange peels to compost.
Believe in systems, insight of patterns, bitter
white webbing of the fruit. This is where hard faith
will get you: blackened with cancers, skywriting
on morphine, announcing our departure as we
degenerate into the heap.

Careful wishing, and scantily clad wants.
Engrossed myself
in taking off his clothes, a pastime,
unshelling his wavering while then and nothing
stood battering the door.

Sick of dying's constancy. Did
you hear me say that? Sick of
this easy spoilage. And yet this life. He will work
this worry, he will fold it in
his fingertips. He is
one hot goodbye.

RECESS

To pursue the odd is to force the door of the ordinary.
No knocking; just entrance and a trip into mundane.

This knowledge colored close to ignorance;
water pressing water.
There is body and form,
there is a presence pausing, a live animal
cleaving to its killer,
a woman waiting for her turn.

There is raw intervention. Plastic of misunderstanding
that slides between her
and all she doesn't know.

The kids won't shut up, despite what we've done to them.
How they holler at recess, crowding the fence.

Before I learned how to write this in English
I wrote it in stones, on my mother's wall.

ANTIETAM

The scope remains the same, only
details have had to shift, like silt,
river bends that heave and change
our way of knowing. In the car,
you learn to focus on the trees ahead
the unchanged map
so flat it looks like anyone
could tear their way across it.

But there were memories of bridges there,
vehicles that stalled and men who pressed
their guts back into torsos
gone concave with ultimatums.

History is pressure on the moment,
not fluidity, not important when we get to
naming days. In the river
our feet disappear in the calcium of Confederate bone.

INCARCERATION

People gave me photos snapped in graveyards
indicating, maybe, that my death-pallor
had not yet improved
even after months of deliberate exposure

there they sat, clenching
those chipped and dirt-veined headstones, knees moist
in new-raked grass, epiphanies
of finding uncles lost in plagues
around the bend of centuries.

People gave me photos from their living rooms,
demonstrating skills at polishing
and staining cabinets;
and notes were tacked onto the images,
bearing a narrative of scavenging
accompanied by height charts of kids I'd never see.

Photographs from prison, only
one arrived: a boy I kissed on Divisadero Street,
who disappeared the next day, victimized
by parking tickets; his glove compartment
erupting pink and tattering.

Cameras lined in pawn shop cases, some were mine;
a way to tuck and run, methods
for boxing up and stilling
the urge for preservation in this not young,
not yet frigid age.

Lux Perpetua

Finally, there is a light
and what it makes of us; so embarrassing we shirk
responsibility, in favor of retreat. What thoughts we had
on passing one another, some afternoon
when randomness meant more than mere association
will remain suppressed. After meeting you it was as if
the notions I had clung to for so long
they might have been foundations were little
more than art and less than time, and you wore on me
enough that I was just raw amber, which will melt
against skin if you press its grains there long enough.

LIONIZATION

Reader, beware. A cuff will come when least
anticipated, the smacking blow a jolt from
expectation. Girl, amazing:
the ways in which you move through time
like nothing scrapes you, not this
ambiguity, not this pose, never this flirting glimpse that skids
then permeates until
you are as focused as a star.

And, upward! An eye will graze a surface pocked
and pitted and see only what shines off of it.
Glances bounce, break, and refract. How busy things are,
making nothing happen fast. Responsibility, betrayal,
histories gouged and re-gouged into a skin
lacquered in emollients so ineffective that their price
wears heavily against their worthiness.

A rumpled bed has meaning. A rumpled face, much less.
Or its meaning is so malleable, so open to interpretation
that gazing upon it translates only to an open text,
a haze of lines, crosshatching and merging in a conversation
that goes on, one way, for years and years. That science that we make
together
is at best a string of observations, perhaps better called a muddle.

Amazing, girl. The manner in which you pull things from a drawer
and layer them upon yourself: not garments
but bits of fretfulness, here one without
meaning beyond its fraying seams; and here another, so sinuous
that the gaze upon it only mutters "dress"
and reels back from its floating hems.

ELEKTRA DREAMS A LIFE

Snow was dirty on the streets: Athens, New York, the way it fell
between the feet that broke the sheets of it, the places
where I slipped and fell, embarrassed the blind man I loved
could move through them with grace I inevitably misunderstood.

I wonder if this earth meant anything, when I leant my form to it;
the first death, the one that stings and separates us.
Imagining it was not mine, I reached out for anyone
who came to me, those faces split so only eyes
could meet mine, where his had been, at best, the darkest blur
I'd ever known. All angles, all in muscles, wrapped up
and girded like a bird tied up so it could mend
when it was, inevitably, broken.

A shoebox on the backseat. I had scooped it up, not noticing
my father kneeling just behind the car, cupping its head
against the outlet of the muffler, so I bandaged it while it was
bent and limp. I believed nothing was inevitable
and I saw only what was literal; the way its feathers
shook and settled, as the car moved on.

Acknowledgements

Some of these poems first appeared in slightly different forms in:

Coconut: "Seven Brides", "Lux Perpetua"
Conduit: "Mule"
Fabula: "Blacklight Series"
InTense: "Reservoir", "Proper Season"
MiPoesias: "Santa Prudencia"
Nidus: "Olympia"
Rooms: "Benign Condescension", "Tertiary", "Percipience"
Shampoo: "Victorians"
6ix: "Sleep, Talk, Believe"
Spinning Jenny: "Seedtime"
Taint: "1988"
Tarpaulin Sky: "Old Dog"
Veer: "Poor", "Wife"
Volt: "Lovers", "Constrictions"

"Rain in May" is for Andy.

"Sleep, Talk, Believe" is for Mosi.

"Victorians" is for Getrude Van Matre Leonard.

"Giants" is for Willie McCovey, Willie Mays, and Candlestick Park.

The Elektra poems owe a debt to Frank Miller's Elektra and Elektra Assassin comics.

This book is for Leo E. Oakes Jr. and Robert Leonard.